# Dream, Little Girl, Dream

Written by Stephanie Green

Illustrated by Lovyaa Garg

This book is a work of fiction. The names, characters and events in this book are the products of the author's imagination or are used fictitiously. Any similarity to real persons living or dead is coincidental and not intended by the author.

Dream, Little Girl, Dream



Edited by: Sharp Editorial



The cover design, interior formatting, typesetting, and editorial work for this book are entirely the product of the author. Gatekeeper Press did not participate in and is not responsible for any aspect of these elements.

ISBN (paperback): 9781662907982

# Dedication

This book was made with love for my daughters, Sofia and Jasmine. I hope you cherish this book forever.

To my loving husband, Jeff, for always helping and pushing me to achieve my goals.

I love you all.

As the sun waved goodbye to the moon, and the moon welcomed the stars into the clear night sky, Sofia and Jasmine knew that bedtime was near.

MIKO
ADVENTURES

"Vamos, Jasmine," Sofia said, prompting her little sister to follow her lead to their bedroom.

"Your dreams are calling," their mother chimed, as she and Papa followed closely behind their daughters' soft footsteps.

Jasmine and Sofia happily cozied into their beds and pulled their fluffy blankets under their tiny chins.

"Buenas noches," Mami said as she kissed each of their foreheads.

"Good night, girls," Papa echoed, giving his daughters one final squeeze.

With one last peek into the room and a final wish for sweet dreams, Mami and Papa quietly closed the bedroom door.

"Sofia," Jasmine whispered, peeking over her fluffy blanket. "Sometimes, I dream of being a ballerina, twirling across the stage in a pretty pink tutu and the crowd bursting into applause."

The sisters giggled, quietly leaving their beds to gracefully twirl around their room like poised ballerinas.

Now wide awake, Sofia and Jasmine plopped on their bedroom floor, giddy with excitement about their sweet dreams.

"I've had dreams of being a famous tennis player," Jasmine shared, "serving the bright yellow ball with all my strength."

"We could be tennis partners, Hermana," Sofia sounded, joining her sister's grand dream of being a star athlete. "Side by side, me and you, playing against another pair."

The two sisters happily sighed
as they continued imagining
where their wildest dreams
could lead.

"Sofia," Jasmine said, interrupting her sister's thoughts. "Have you ever dreamed of being a teacher?"

"Si," Sofia happily answered. "I've dreamed about a colorful classroom full of eager, curious faces. 'Mrs. Green,' the students would call as they raise their hands high to answer my questions."

Jasmine grinned. "Hermana, you would be a wonderful teacher."

"Good morning, class. Today, we will learn about outer space," Sofia said, penciling on her imaginary chalkboard.

"Good morning, Ms. Green," Jasmine giggled, playing along with her sister's vivid imagination.

As Sofia walked toward Jasmine, returning her pencil to its rightful place, she bumped her foot on the corner of her towering dresser.

"Ouch!" Sofia grimaced as small tears formed in the corners of her eyes.

Noticing her sister's pain, Jasmine quickly motioned for Sofia to sit. "No llores, Hermana," Jasmine softly said, wiping the tears from Sofia's eyes. "For a moment, let's dream I am your doctor, ready to care for you."

With a few pretend stitches and a hug from little sister, Sofia was feeling better and ready to explore dreamland again.

Suddenly, Sofia and Jasmine heard footsteps approaching their bedroom door.
"Mami, Papa!" they whispered as they rushed and jumped into bed, pretending to be asleep as they should have been.

The door slowly opened, and Mami and Papa couldn't help but smile at the sight of their little dreamers. "Dream, little girls, dream," Mami said, poking her head into the room, bringing an end to the girls' evening of pretend.

"And may your dreams be sweet, indeed."

The end

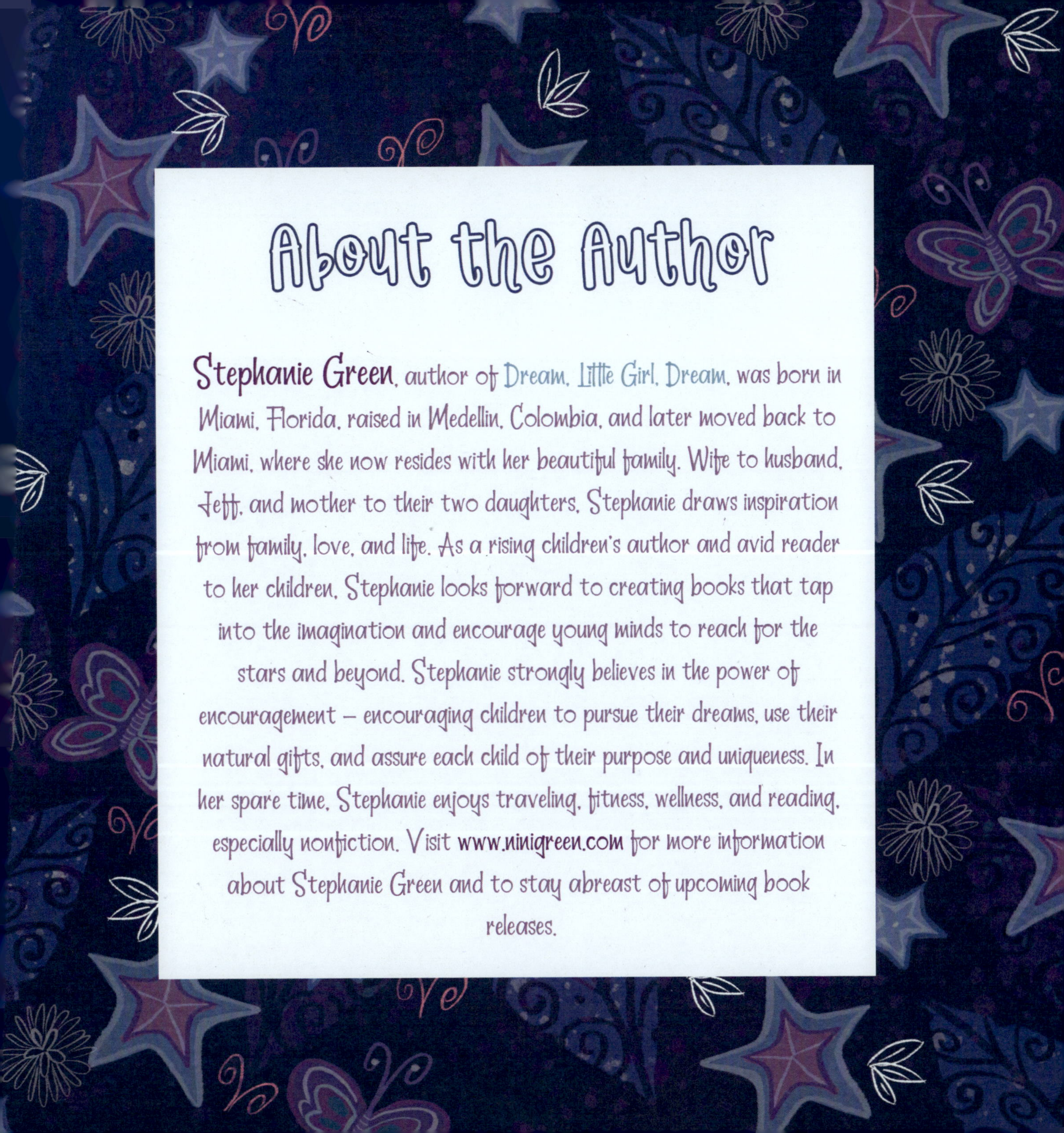

# About the Author

Stephanie Green, author of Dream, Little Girl, Dream, was born in Miami, Florida, raised in Medellin, Colombia, and later moved back to Miami, where she now resides with her beautiful family. Wife to husband, Jeff, and mother to their two daughters, Stephanie draws inspiration from family, love, and life. As a rising children's author and avid reader to her children, Stephanie looks forward to creating books that tap into the imagination and encourage young minds to reach for the stars and beyond. Stephanie strongly believes in the power of encouragement – encouraging children to pursue their dreams, use their natural gifts, and assure each child of their purpose and uniqueness. In her spare time, Stephanie enjoys traveling, fitness, wellness, and reading, especially nonfiction. Visit www.ninigreen.com for more information about Stephanie Green and to stay abreast of upcoming book releases.